What to Do When Your
TEMPER
FLARES

A Kid's Guide
to Overcoming
Problems with Anger

by Dawn Huebner, Ph.D.

illustrated by Bonnie Matthews

MAGINATION PRESS • WASHINGTON, D.C.

Published by
MAGINATION PRESS®
An Educational Publishing Foundation Book
American Psychological Association
750 First Street, NE
Washington, DC 20002

Magination Press is a registered trademark of the American Psychological Association.
For more information about our books, including a complete catalog, please write to us,
call 1-800-374-2721, or visit our website at www.maginationpress.com.

Library of Congress Cataloging-in-Publication Data

Huebner, Dawn.
What to do when your temper flares : a kid's guide to overcoming problems with anger /
by Dawn Huebner ; illustrated by Bonnie Matthews.
p.   cm. — (What-to-do guides for kids)
Summary: "Teaches school-age children cognitive-behavioral techniques to manage anger,
through writing and drawing activities and self-help exercises and strategies.
Includes introduction for parents" —Provided by publisher.
ISBN-13: 978-1-4338-0134-1 (pbk. : alk. paper)
ISBN-10: 1-4338-0134-5 (pbk. : alk. paper)
1. Anger—Juvenile literature.
I. Matthews, Bonnie, ill. II. Title. III. Series.
BF575.A5H84 2007
155.4'1247—dc22   2007012036

Manufactured in the United States of America
10 9 8

CONTENTS

Introduction to Parents and Caregivers

Fireworks! We eagerly head out to see them each year. Something about the suddenness—the sharp crack preceding the explosion of light—has us holding our breath, anticipating the next one, and the next one, and the next. We peer up into the darkness with a certain tension in our bodies, watching, waiting. And then comes the dazzling display.

It's one thing to watch fireworks from a patch of grass, craning our necks upward, knowing that the bursts and their fizzling remains are far away. It's quite another to witness them day after day inside our own homes, to be singed by the explosions that take place within our walls. Yet this is the experience of parents whose children have problems with anger.

If you are reading this book, chances are good that you love a child whose anger alarms you. Perhaps your child is easily set off, flaring at the slightest provocation. Perhaps your child is aggressive, lashing out with fists or with words. Or maybe you see your child years from now, still unable to cope with setbacks, making bad situations worse, alienating family and friends. Your concern is understandable. Elementary school-age

children with short fuses are unlikely to magically outgrow this problem. The combination of genetics, temperament, and learning conspire to set behaviors in place, leading to a pattern of explosiveness that can extend over the course of a lifetime. No one wants this for their child.

As tempting as it might be to look for a way to squelch or erase your child's anger, that is not the cure you will find in these pages. Anger is, after all, a normal, healthy feeling. While not particularly pleasant, it is our body's way of alerting us to problems. Anger fuels us, giving us the energy we need to right wrongs. But, as you know, it comes with a pretty major downside. Anger can get too big, raging out of control in the blink of an eye. It can be misdirected or expressed in hurtful ways. So while we do not want to be sending our children the message that they shouldn't feel angry, we do want to help them learn to harness their anger, to use it in constructive (rather than destructive) ways.

Children tend to experience anger as something that happens to them. They don't like what someone says or does and—BAM! —they're angry. *What to Do When Your Temper Flares* helps children turn around this passive response to anger. It teaches them a new way to think about anger, along with a set of tools they can use to turn down the heat and respond more appropriately when something goes wrong.

The techniques described in this book are based on cognitive-behavioral principles. The cognitive piece helps children understand and gain control over their

4

thoughts. The behavioral piece teaches a set of constructive skills. The aim is to go beyond simply reading about managing anger to actually doing it. So *What to Do When Your Temper Flares* builds on the knowledge, strengths, and motivation children already possess, helping them feel competent right from the start. New concepts are tacked on to familiar ones; new skills are taught step-by-step, in ways that are manageable and fun. Practice is built into the program.

You play an important role in helping your child learn and use the skills described in this book. Take the time to preview the book. You will be a more effective guide if you know where you and your child are going. While your child might be capable of reading this book alone, it is much more helpful for children to read it together with a parent (or other supportive adult). Make working on the book a priority, without distractions pulling you away. Take turns reading paragraphs. Stop for your child to do the drawing and writing exercises as they appear.

You are undoubtedly eager for your child to get a handle on his or her anger. Avoid the temptation, however, to race your child through this book. Children benefit most if they have time to absorb the ideas and practice the skills contained within these pages. So read slowly, just one or two chapters at a time. Between reading sessions, use the language you and your child are learning. Refer to the metaphors often, helping your child link them to his or her actual experiences. Use humor as it is modeled here, gently, with you and your child always on the same side of the joke. Be patient. It takes time and practice to

remember new skills and use them smoothly.

You can help your child practice the anger-dousing methods that make up the bulk of this book by practicing them yourself. All of the techniques are as relevant to adults as they are to children. Life will be happier and more peaceful if everyone in the family is using them. If it is difficult for you or someone else in your family to remain calm in the face of your child's anger, please seek the help of a professional to guide you through this program.

Children (and adults) can learn a set of skills to tame anger—to calm down, think clearly, solve problems, and ultimately move on. Teaching children these skills is tremendously important, as children who show good self-control tend to be better liked by peers, more successful academically, and easier to live with, not to mention just plain happier. And you will be happier, too. *What to Do When Your Temper Flares* will help your child move the fireworks back outside, where they belong, as bursts of color in the nighttime sky.

CHAPTER ONE

In the Driver's Seat

Have you ever driven a car?

If your answer is yes, let's hope you're talking about a bumper car at an amusement park, or a battery-run car in your driveway, or one of those remote control vehicles that race around the floor of your house. When you're older, you'll learn to drive a real car.

◎ Draw yourself driving your dream car, one that you hope to own someday.

Driving is fun. You get to decide where to go, and you're in charge of getting there.

It's also hard work. You have to pay attention all the time. You have to steer. You have to turn just the right amount, not too much or too little. You have to speed up, but not too fast. You have to avoid all the other cars around you. You have to follow the rules. It's easy to lose control and then CRASH!

It's fun to crash a bumper car. That's what they're made for anyway. And it's fun to crash a remote control car, especially the kind that's designed to climb walls and flip over.

But in a real car, it isn't fun to crash. It's scary and dangerous and can lead to bad things. That's why people need to take lessons before they drive a real car. And one of the main things you learn when you take driving lessons is to stay in control of the car.

Our bodies are kind of like cars. We need fuel to run well. We need to be kept clean. We need to get checkups every once in a while. And we need to follow rules that help keep everyone safe.

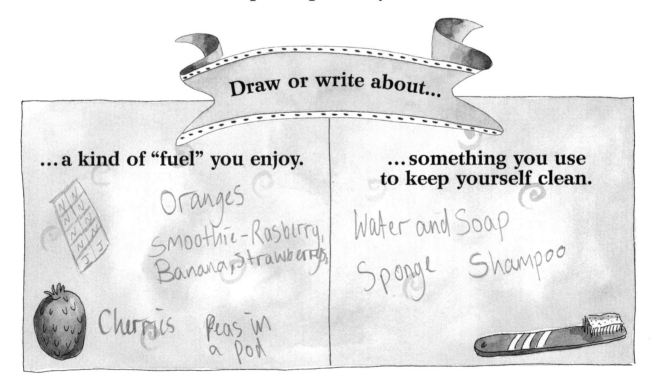

Draw or write about...

...a kind of "fuel" you enjoy.

Oranges
Smoothie-Rasberry, Banana, Strawberry
Cherries   Peas in a Pod

...something you use to keep yourself clean.

Water and Soap
Sponge   Shampoo

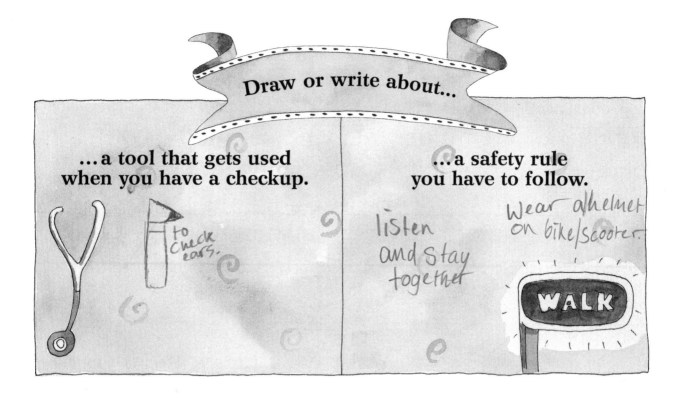

Draw or write about...

...a tool that gets used when you have a checkup.

to check ears.

...a safety rule you have to follow.

listen and stay together

Wear a helmet on bike/scooter.

WALK

When you're driving, sometimes there are no other cars on the road, and the road is straight, and you know exactly where you're going. All of these things make it easy to follow the rules and stay in control of the car.

But sometimes the road is crowded or bumpy or full of turns. Sometimes you're in a hurry or tired or lost. Sometimes it's windy or foggy or so dark you can hardly see, even with your lights on.

HONK HONK

Good drivers know that under all of these conditions, even if they're in a bad mood or their phone is ringing or kids are arguing, even if other cars are driving too close or cutting them off, even if it's snowing or raining, no matter what, they still need to stay in control of the car. Otherwise, there could be a disaster.

You have a few years to go before you get behind the wheel of a real car, but you can still learn how to be a good driver. You can practice on yourself.

That's right, you get to be in the driver's seat of your own life, right now, starting today.

Sometimes it's easy to be in control of yourself, and it's fun, too. You can decide how loud to sing or how high to jump or what book to take out of the library. But sometimes it isn't fun. Sometimes there are rules you don't want to follow. Sometimes you want something but you can't have it. Sometimes people do things you don't want them to do, and say things you don't want them to say.

Yet you are still the driver, not in charge of other people, but in charge of steering and controlling yourself. And just like the driver of a real car, the things you do and the choices you make determine what kind of trip you're going to have.

Maybe your trip has been rocky, making it difficult for you to stay in control. Maybe you're a kid who gets overheated when things go wrong, a kid who tries to cool down but ends up exploding instead. Well, guess what? You don't have to be that kind of kid much longer.

If you're a kid who's ready to learn to be the driver in your own life, to control yourself even when it's hard, this book is for you. It will teach you how to avoid crashes and get where you want to go.

CHAPTER TWO

A Secret About Anger

Everyone gets angry sometimes. In fact, it's such a common feeling that we have lots of words to describe it. Here are some words that all mean ANGRY. See if you can think of a few more.

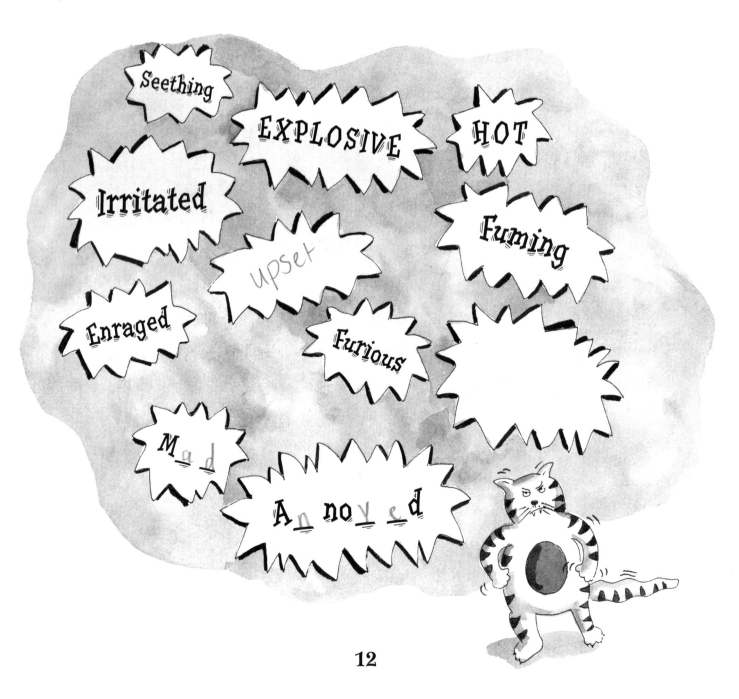

Seething

EXPLOSIVE

HOT

Irritated

Fuming

Upset

Enraged

Furious

Mad

Annoyed

Think about what it feels like to be angry. Make an angry face to help yourself get in the mood. Try to bring the actual feeling into your body. It doesn't feel very good, does it?

Now think about all the times when someone has been mad at you. That doesn't feel very good either. In fact, when you think about it, it probably seems like anger is something to be avoided.

But actually, anger is a good thing. It's our body's way of telling us that we don't like what's going on.

The problem is, it can get big so fast.

It can cause us to say things we don't really mean and do things we would never do if we were calm and in control. Anger that has gotten too big can make bad situations even worse, and get us into lots and lots of trouble.

Think of some things that have made you mad recently. Think carefully. Think about school and home. Think about your little brother and your big sister. Think about the things you want that you can't have. Think about the things people sometimes say and do that drive you nuts. Think about the last time you yelled at your mom or dad. Think hard, and make your list here.

Things That Make Me
MAD

People Saying that I like Kairn and Murry keeps on saying annoying things

Mum Saying to dad that She wanted Some time away from him.

Grandma having a Stroke

When you arrange Something that your excited about and then get told it's not happining

Did you write down lots of things that make you mad? Most kids do. There are so many things that lead to angry feelings.

But there's a secret about anger, something that will save you from exploding when something goes wrong. Once you know this secret, your anger won't get so big, so scary, or so likely to get you into trouble anymore. (By the way, lots of adults don't know this secret either, which is why they get so mad so often, too.)

THE ONLY THING THAT MAKES YOU ANGRY IS YOU.

If you're like most kids, learning this little secret might make you kind of mad. You might be thinking, "This book is stupid. I don't make myself mad! It's my pesky brother or my mean teacher or my sister hogging the computer…or whatever."

Hang in there, though. Take a deep breath. Grab a marker. You are about to learn something really, really interesting, something that might even change your life.

⊚ Draw someone (not yourself) taking the last cookie from this plate.

That would make you mad, wouldn't it? What might you be thinking?

⊚ Write your ideas in the empty bubbles.

⊚ Fill in the face to show how you would feel.

But what if these thoughts were in your head instead:

If these were your thoughts, how might you be feeling?

◎ Fill in the face above to show the feeling.

You see, it isn't what happened that made you mad. Both ways, someone had taken the last cookie. Instead, it was your *thoughts* about what happened that made you mad, or that helped you feel fine.

Let's try another one.

Next week is school vacation. Your teacher is concerned about the class falling behind, so she includes 30 words on this week's spelling list, instead of the usual 20. What might you be thinking that would make you mad?

 Write it down.

Okay, here's the exact same situation, only let's change the thoughts.

What are some thoughts you might think that could help you deal with having 10 extra words?

◎ Write one of those thoughts down.

OH WELL, IT'S JUST 2 EXTRA WORDS A DAY, AND BESIDES, THERE WON'T BE ANY WORDS NEXT WEEK

PURR PURR

If I can do them all today I'll have more time to PLAY!

So it isn't what happens that makes you mad. It's what you *think* about what happens that determines how you feel.

Now, you already know that you can't control what happens to you. People say things and do things without asking your permission. It rains on the day of your pool party, or you lose at Go Fish, or someone teases you at school. You can't control any of those things.

But you can control what you think, and what you think determines how you feel. So if you change your thoughts, you can change your feelings. And if you're tired of being a kid who blows up whenever something doesn't go your way, all you have to do is learn how to move away from the angry thoughts that are causing those explosions.

It's something lots of kids have learned to do, and you can, too.

Keep reading and you will learn how.

Does Anger Win You Friends?

It's going to take some effort on your part to learn to change your thoughts to stay in better control of your anger. You might be wondering, "Why bother?"

It's a good question.

@ Take a minute to answer these questions:

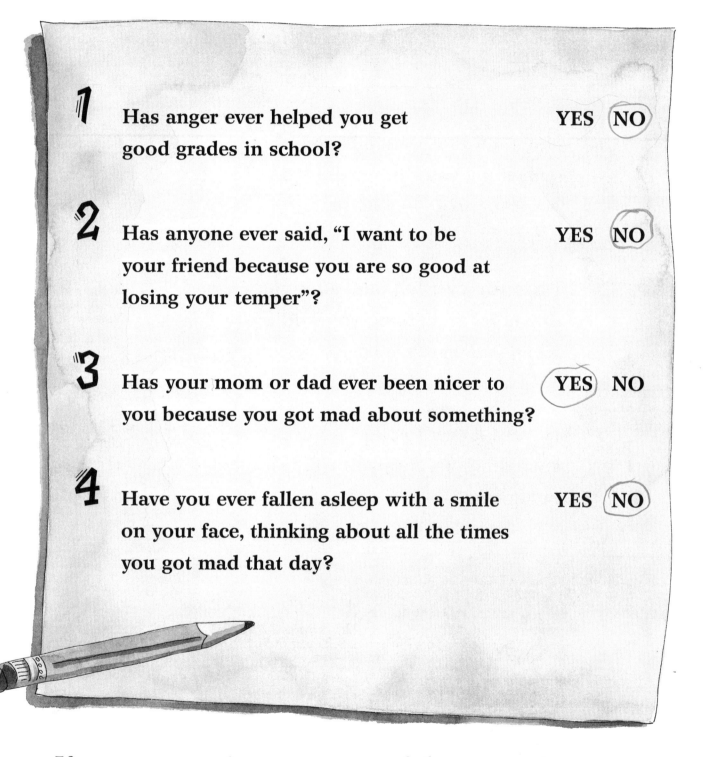

1 Has anger ever helped you get good grades in school?　　　YES (NO)

2 Has anyone ever said, "I want to be your friend because you are so good at losing your temper"?　　　YES (NO)

3 Has your mom or dad ever been nicer to you because you got mad about something?　　　(YES) NO

4 Have you ever fallen asleep with a smile on your face, thinking about all the times you got mad that day?　　　YES (NO)

If your answer is no to most of these questions, then anger isn't helping you out in any way.

@ Now answer these questions:

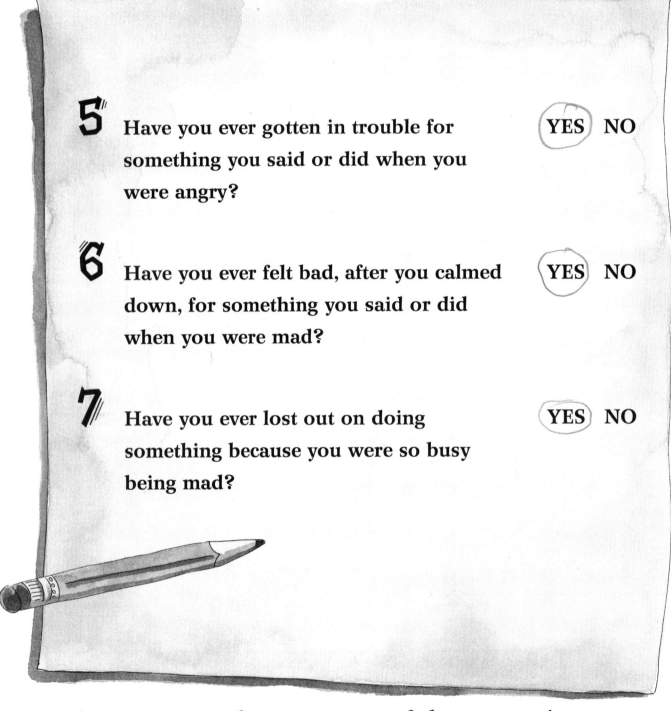

5 Have you ever gotten in trouble for something you said or did when you were angry? (YES) NO

6 Have you ever felt bad, after you calmed down, for something you said or did when you were mad? (YES) NO

7 Have you ever lost out on doing something because you were so busy being mad? (YES) NO

If you answered yes to most of these questions, anger is not only *not* helping you, it is actually making things worse.

Anger doesn't win you friends or make things easier for you at home. In fact, it's probably causing you lots of trouble. That's why it's a good idea to learn to tame your anger, so it can stop causing you so much trouble.

You might be thinking that if other people would just stop bugging you, you would be fine. And you might be right about that. But the thing is, you can't control what other people do.

That's the bad news. You can't control what other people do.

But the good news is that you can be happy anyway. You can learn to control your own temper, even if other people are bugging you or making things tough. And kids who are in control of their anger are generally happier kids.

CHAPTER FOUR

Fire! Fire!

People often say that anger is like fire. It's **HOT**. It can **RAGE** out of control. It **BURNS** anyone who gets too close. It's a good comparison, so let's talk about fire for a minute.

Even if you have never actually built a fire, you probably know how it's done. You need some wood, arranged so the air can flow through. You need some tinder, like twigs or crumpled pieces of paper. The tinder is the stuff that will quickly catch fire. And then you need something to get the fire started, maybe a match.

◎ Build a fire in this stone pit.

If you want the flames to blaze higher and last a long, long time, what would you need to do?

Adding more wood to the fire will keep it going. Creating a short, swift breeze by fanning or blowing on it will help the fire, too. Tending the fire by adding to it is called *feeding* a fire.

But what if you want the fire to go out? What would you need to do?

If you leave the fire alone by not blowing on it or adding any more wood, the fire will eventually run out of fuel. And with nothing left to burn, the fire will go out. If you want to put the fire out faster, you need to pour water on it, sometimes lots of water. This is called *dousing* a fire. Water extinguishes the flames and soaks the wood, making it hard to burn.

Anger really is a lot like fire, isn't it? Sometimes all it takes is one little thing to get it going. Anger can flare up and burn out quickly, or it can turn into a roaring blaze that wrecks everything in its path.

And as you will see, whether anger flares up or fizzles out is totally up to you.

When things happen that make you mad, you have a choice. You can feed your anger, or you can douse it.

You already know how to feed anger. All you have to do is think lots of angry thoughts, and your anger will get bigger and bigger. Angry actions, like hitting someone or tearing something up, make anger get bigger, too.

But what about dousing anger? How in the world can you do that? Actually, there are lots of ways.

Each of the next four chapters will teach you an anger-dousing method. Learn them one by one, and then decide which methods work best for you.

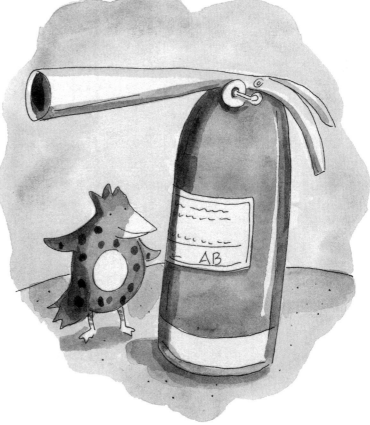

Anger-Dousing Method #1: Take a Break

Being angry is like standing in front of a giant vacuum cleaner.

If you're reading this book at home, go find your vacuum cleaner so you can do an experiment. (Ask your mom or dad first, to make sure it's okay.) If you aren't near a vacuum cleaner, keep reading anyway. You can use your imagination, and your knowledge of vacuum cleaners, to help you understand this experiment.

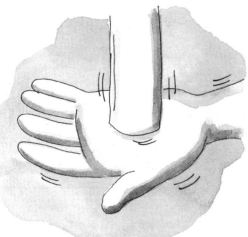

Attach the hose to the vacuum cleaner, and turn it on. Put the palm of your hand in front of the hose. What do you feel?

It's powerful, isn't it?

Leave the vacuum cleaner on and move your hand away from the hose, all the way to the side of it. What do you feel now? (Nothing, right?)

Now move your hand back in front of the hose. Yikes! That's strong, isn't it?

What if there was a giant vacuum cleaner with a giant hose turned on, right in front of you? It would suck you right in, wouldn't it?

What if you didn't want to be sucked into the vacuum cleaner? What would you need to do?

If you didn't want to get sucked into the vacuum cleaner, you would have two choices:

1 **Reach up and turn the vacuum cleaner off.**

2 **Move out of the way before its pull gets too strong.**

Anger is like that giant vacuum cleaner. It will grab you and hold on tight. By the time you finish reading this book, you'll know how to turn anger off. But for now let's talk about your other choice: Move out of the way.

The way to get out of anger's way is to take a break.

Taking a break means walking away from the scene of your anger. It means going off by yourself so you can calm down and think more clearly. It is a very, very helpful thing to do, but it's also a hard thing to do.

Why is that?

Think about the giant vacuum cleaner again. The longer you stand in front of it, the more it's going to pull you in and the harder it will be to break away. You have to be really determined and strong to decide "I'm outta here!" and step out of its path. But once you do, things become a whole lot easier. As soon as you step away, you break the vacuum cleaner's hold on you.

Anger is like that, too. You have to make a decision to step aside. That doesn't mean you're giving in. It just means you're taking a break. There are lots of ways to take a break.

You can go to your room.

You can shoot some baskets.

You can read a book.

You can let your pet lizard crawl up your arm.

You can even take a break at school by going to get a drink of water or drawing a picture of your favorite cartoon character on a spare piece of paper.

What are four things you can do while
taking a break from an angry situation?

Draw or write
about them here.

Count to

30

Go to some-
where quiet and
Breath in and
out.

Talk to
your cat or
Rabbit

listen to
music
(A tune thats
your favorite)

As you're learning new ways to deal with anger, it's important to practice a lot. There is a fun way to keep track of your practice taking a break.

Find a long piece of yarn or string and put it in your room, if your room is the main place you'll be going to take a break. Each time you step away from the force of your anger, go to your room, and do something fun or relaxing while you calm down, tie one knot in the string.

When you have 10 knots, show your mom and dad so they can celebrate with you. Decide ahead of time what your 10-knot celebration might be: a board game before bed, an ice cream outing, a sleepover with a friend.

◎ Write your ideas by the knotted piece of string.

After you have 10 knots, try for 20.
Then 30.

When you start to feel angry,
think about that giant
vacuum cleaner pulling you in.
Don't just stand there!
Decide to step out
of its way.
Go take a break.

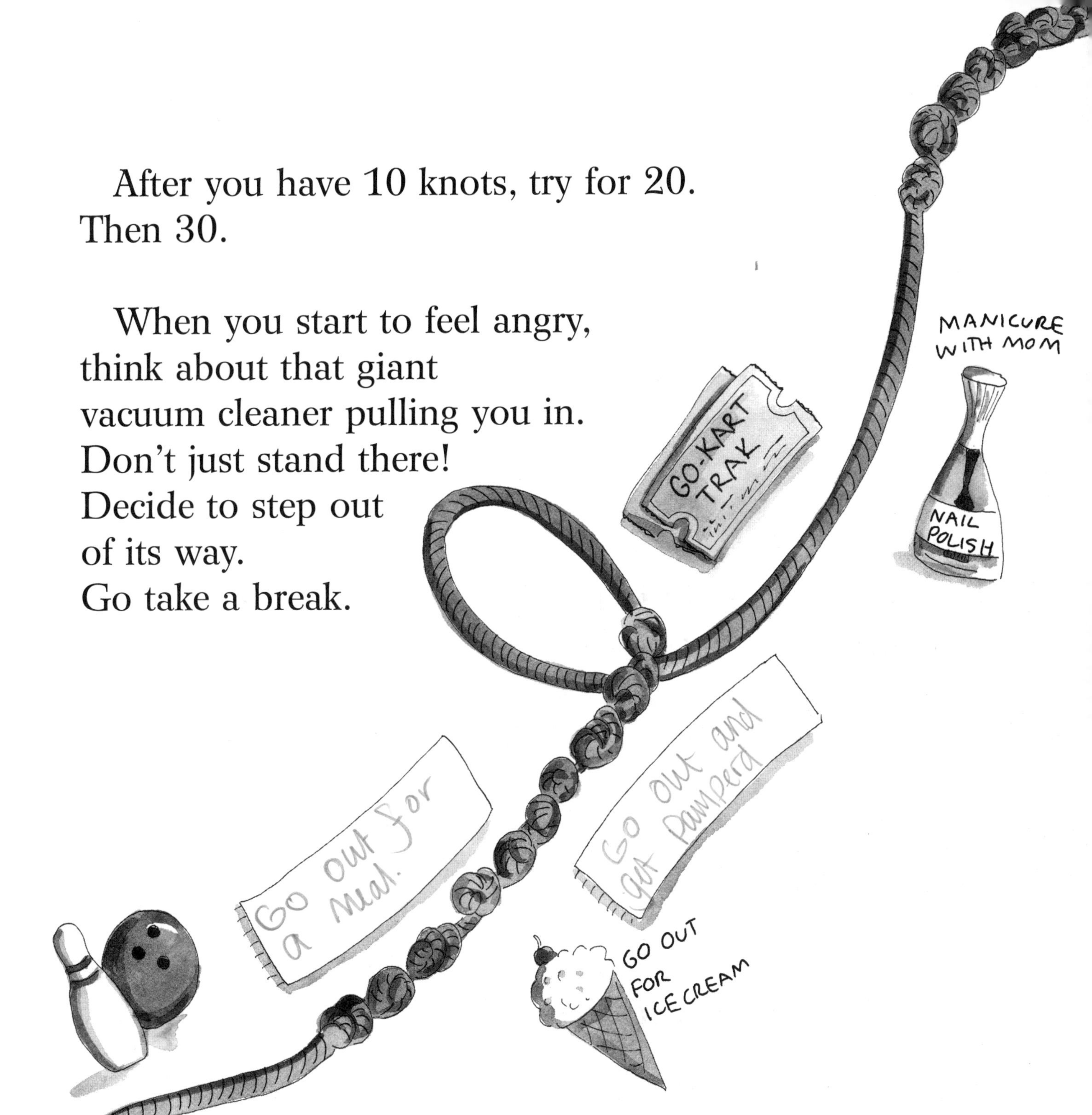

MANICURE
WITH MOM

GO-KART
TRAK

NAIL
POLISH

Go out for
a meal.

Go out and
get pampered

GO OUT
FOR
ICE CREAM

Taking a break helps you feel better so you can
think more clearly. When you're thinking clearly,
you're less likely to get in trouble and more likely
to come up with a solution to what's bothering
you. Try it, you'll see.

Anger-Dousing Method #2: Think Cool Thoughts

Have you ever noticed that you talk to yourself? Everyone does. It's like there's a tiny voice inside each of us commenting on what we see, what just happened, what's coming up next. This tiny voice is really our thoughts, not something separate from us, but an important part of who we are.

Some people are aware of this tiny voice. If you ask what they're thinking, they can tell you. Other people aren't so aware of it. If you ask what they're thinking, they'll shrug or they'll say they weren't thinking anything. But everyone's brain is busy all the time churning out thoughts, whether we realize it or not.

WHAT PAGE ARE WE ON?

I CAN'T WAIT TO RIDE MY BIKE

I'M SO HUNGRY! I WANT...

I WANT TO PLAY NOW

When we're angry, the first thoughts our brains churn out are usually HOT ones. For most people, this happens automatically. They get mad, and then they start thinking about and talking to themselves about being mad. As you might imagine, these hot thoughts actually keep anger going. They are the tinder that feeds the fire of anger.

Here are some examples of hot thoughts:

Read each situation that's described below. Write down the first hot thought that pops into your mind.

You are playing your favorite video game and losing big time.

Swear in my head

Why didn't you listen to me?

Your mother gave you broccoli for dinner last night, and you told her you hated it. She just put broccoli on your plate again.

You are working on math problems at school. You get to one that you have no idea how to solve.

Think of Strategys.

Your friend, who promised to play with you at recess today, runs off with someone else instead.

Each of these hot thoughts is guaranteed to make your anger worse. Hot thoughts feed anger, making it grow.

Taking a break, which you learned about in the last chapter, gives you a chance to calm down.

It's like walking away from a small fire. As long as you don't keep thinking hot thoughts during your break, your anger will fizzle, and eventually it will go out. Then you will be able to deal with the problem more effectively.

But there is something you can do to put the fire out sooner. You can think *COOL* thoughts.

Cool thoughts are things you can say inside your own head to feel better. Cool thoughts don't tell you what to do, but they do calm you down. The point of cool thoughts is to sprinkle water on the hot thoughts, lowering the heat.

Here are some examples of cool thoughts:

Kids often try to simply ignore their hot thoughts. As you know, that doesn't work very well. But cool thoughts do work well. They are different from ignoring because they are much more active. Cool thoughts put out the fire of hot thoughts.

I CAN DEAL WITH THIS

THIS ISN'T WORTH GETTING ANGRY ABOUT

WHATEVER

@ Read each example below. Write a cool thought in the bubble. You can look back to pages 42 and 43 for ideas, or make up a cool thought of your own.

You just struck out at bat.

At least I got to play in the game

At least I will just say sorry to Mum and go to my room.

Your mom yells at you for teasing your brother, but he started it.

You can't find your homework, and the bus will be here any minute.

Where did I see it last.

You are really thirsty and you want to stop for a drink, but your dad says he's not stopping.

Here's something really interesting about cool thoughts. They only work when you think them yourself. When someone says a cool thought to you, it doesn't help much at all. In fact, it often makes things worse. So if you're getting mad, your parents shouldn't try to say the cool thoughts for you. Instead, they can say, "It looks like you're getting angry. What hot thoughts are in your head right now? What cool thoughts can you tell yourself so you can start to feel better?"

Saying cool thoughts to yourself works surprisingly well. Cool thoughts even help if you don't fully believe them. In fact, the more you tell yourself a cool thought, the more true it becomes.

For example, pretend you're going to the aquarium with your class, and you got paired up with a kid you don't really like. Hot thoughts might come bursting into your head:

Are your hot thoughts likely to magically change your partner? No!

Are your hot thoughts likely to help you enjoy the field trip? No!

But cool thoughts will help. So you remember what you've been reading, and you think the cool thought:

You might need to say it a few times. You might need to tell yourself to calm down and take some deep breaths. You might need to take a brief break, maybe by shifting your thoughts to all of the amazing fish you're going to see.

You can't help the hot thoughts that automatically pop into your head. But you can decide not to keep these hot thoughts going. If you move away from them, and especially if you replace them with cool thoughts, you will start to feel better.

And the truth is, you will survive, even though you didn't get the partner you wanted. Not only will you survive, but you'll get stronger. You'll see that you can deal with disappointments and upsets. You can steer around them or right through them without anything terrible happening. And bad situations end a whole lot quicker when you aren't busy making them worse with your anger.

Anger-Dousing Method #3: Release Anger Safely

Our brains and bodies work together to keep us safe. When a hockey puck comes flying toward us or a kid on roller blades comes barreling down the sidewalk, our brains quickly tell our bodies to get ready for action. We can duck down or spring out of the way or do whatever we might need to do to protect ourselves.

Our brains see anger the same way they see flying hockey pucks. DANGER! When we get angry, an alarm goes off inside our bodies.

WHACK!

Our hearts start beating faster and our muscles get ready for action, in case we need to defend ourselves. Angry thoughts fuel our body's reaction, just like wood fuels a fire. The more angry thoughts we have, the hotter and tighter and angrier we feel.

For some kids, anger moves quickly from something they are thinking about to something their whole body is feeling. They breathe differently, in a more shallow way. Their muscles tighten up, and a charge of energy goes through them, making them feel like they could explode. Kids with this kind of body anger feel like they have to *do* something, to kick or smash or rip something to pieces, to get the angry energy out.

It's a terrible feeling to have anger trapped inside like that. Cooling thoughts help, but sometimes they aren't enough. When anger has made its way into your whole body, it needs to be released to help your body feel okay again.

Some kids try to release their anger by doing something angry.

They shout out angry words.

Or they do hurtful things.

But kids who release in these ways find that their anger still feels pretty big and pretty awful. That's because these things aren't really releases. They are expressions of anger, which means that they show anger, but don't really do anything for you (except probably get you into trouble).

People sometimes recommend "safe" ways to show anger, like punching a pillow or screaming silently. If you have tried these methods, you have probably discovered that they don't work very well either. That's because they are still angry actions, so while you're doing them, your brain is still ROARING and your body is still churning up all that angry energy.

You need something more than a show. You need an actual release, one that gets the anger out without hurting anyone or anything, one that isn't going to get you into trouble or make you feel bad later.

There are two different ways to get this kind of release. One involves moving your body fast, to burn up all that angry energy. The other involves slowing your body down, to snuff the anger out. Here's how each method works.

Active Method

You already know that anger is like fuel in your body. To get rid of it, you have to burn it off. One of the ways to burn off angry energy is physical activity, the faster the better. Hop on your bike and race around the block. Do jumping jacks. Go running with your dog. Crank up some music and dance.

This method works best if you're focused on the activity itself or on something totally unrelated to whatever you were angry about. So count in your head, or imagine yourself in an adventure story with your favorite superhero, or sing (loudly!), or say a word over and over again.

Remember that this method is different from taking a break. Taking a break in a quiet way like playing a video game or reading a book isn't going to help you if anger is charging through your whole body. To release the anger in your body, think in terms of getting your heart to beat fast. Think about exercising your muscles and breaking a sweat. Think about something that will take at least 10 or 15 minutes to do. Activity, especially if it's fun, will burn the angry energy out of your system, leaving you feeling good inside.

It's helpful to think ahead about the active things you can do in each of the places where anger causes trouble for you. Maybe you can get permission from your teacher to run up and down the stairs at school. Maybe you can use your parents' exercise bike at home. Maybe you can clear a path to run around your house outside.

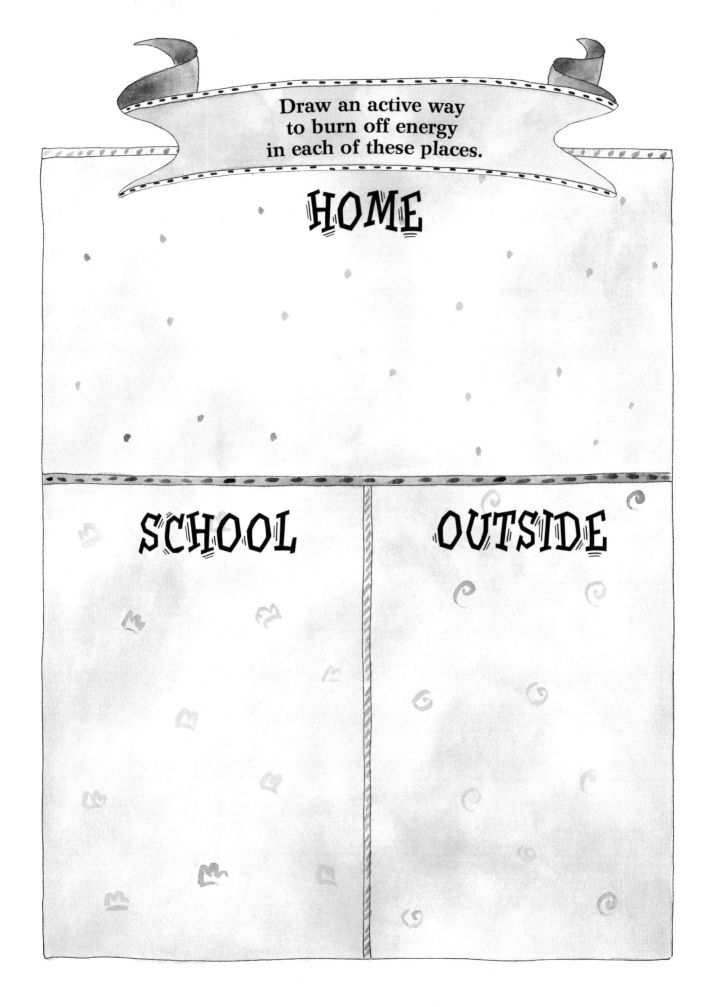

Draw an active way
to burn off energy
in each of these places.

HOME

SCHOOL

OUTSIDE

Slowing Down Method

When energy is racing through your body, you can either do something active to burn it off, or you can do something quiet to slow things down. Slowing down methods are relaxing and private. They are also totally portable, which means you can do them anytime, anywhere.

Breathing is an important part of each of the slowing down methods. Breathing deeply helps to slow down your heart, making you feel better inside. So let's learn about breathing first.

Everyone knows how to breathe. You do it all the time without thinking about it. But there are actually lots of different ways to breathe. You can take air in through your nose, or you can take it in through your mouth. You can also let it out through your nose or your mouth. You can take short, panting breaths high up in your chest, or you can take in deep lungfuls of air. Experiment with breathing a few different ways.

The best slowing-your-body-down kind of breathing starts by closing your mouth and taking a good, full breath in through your nose, the kind of in-breath you might take if you walked into a bakery and smelled cookies just out of the oven. As you breathe in, count slowly to 3 in your head.

To breathe out, keep your mouth closed and let the air back out through your nose. If you're used to breathing through your mouth, this might seem a bit tricky. Try it a few times so you can get the hang of it. As you breathe out, count slowly to 4 in your head, so that the out-breath is a little longer than the in-breath.

After each breath, pause for a moment, and then start the next breath. Remember to go in through your nose (counting 1-2-3) and out through your nose (1-2-3-4). If you need to open your mouth a little to let more air out, that's okay. Just remember to close your mouth again for the in-breath.

Some kids like to imagine something as they breathe in and out. With each breath in, you can imagine yourself breathing in your favorite smell. Breathe in _____ (write your favorite smell here) and breathe out all of your hot, angry feelings. Imagine the anger leaving your body as you slowly fill up with your favorite smell.

Other kids like to focus on counting, clearing their minds of everything but the numbers as they keep track of their breath going in and out, in and out.

Either way is fine. The important thing is to let go of whatever is making you angry so you can just breathe...breathe...breathe.

The second part of the slowing down method gets the rest of your body involved. Try each of these three choices, and see which you like best.

Choice 1: Stretch

Stretch your arms way up over your head. Reach with your fingertips for the ceiling, as high as you can go. Breathe in (1-2-3) and out (1-2-3-4).

Put your hands on your shoulders with your elbows pointed out. Breathe in as you twist slowly to one side. Breathe out as you twist to the other side. Twist back and forth, gently stretching your body with each twist. Keep breathing (in 1-2-3…out 1-2-3-4).

Clasp your hands behind your back. Bend forward while you bring your arms up, behind you, stretching gently to raise your arms toward the ceiling. Breathe in (1-2-3) and out (1-2-3-4) twice.

Straighten up and drop your hands to your sides. Roll your head gently to one side, then the other, back and forth. Keep breathing.

Choice 2: Squeeze

Grab a pillow, and suck in a big lungful of air (through your nose, remember).

While you're breathing in, squeeze the pillow as tightly as you can. Even if it's a small pillow, put your whole body into the squeeze. Tighten your arms around the pillow,

scrunch up your face, and stiffen the muscles in your legs. Keep your whole body in that giant squeeze while you count 1-2-3 in your head.

Next, loosen your grip on the pillow and relax everything while you breathe out, counting 1-2-3-4.

While you're relaxed, take a slow, deep breath in (counting 1-2-3) and out (counting 1-2-3-4).

Then breathe in and squeeze again.

Go through this pattern five times: breathe in, squeeze and hold, release and breathe out, breathe in and out one time without squeezing, then start again.

Choice 3: Tap

Cross your arms to make an X across your chest.

Tap your right shoulder with your left hand, and then your left shoulder with your right hand. As you tap, count in your head. Tap once for each number you say to yourself.

Breathe slowly, but don't count your breaths. Count your taps instead.

Keep going—right, left, right, left, right, left— tapping back and forth, over and over again, until you get to 100.

Keep your arms crossed and take two extra breaths, slow and relaxing, in and out through your nose.
In 1-2-3...out 1-2-3-4...pause.
In 1-2-3...out 1-2-3-4...pause.

Then start tapping again.
Tap, tap, tap, tap,
until you get to 100.

Slowing down methods work best if you practice them first when you aren't angry. For the next week, practice your favorite slowing down method every day for 5 or 10 minutes. Practice at a time when you're just hanging around, not when you're mad.

The week after that, do something really active for 10 minutes to get your heart beating fast, then practice your favorite slowing down method. Practicing this way will help you learn to actually slow down your heart and calm your body, which is exactly what you'll need to do when you're mad.

Practicing might seem a little boring to you. Some kids try to skip this step. But the methods won't work as well if you haven't practiced first. Maybe you can get one of your parents to practice with you. (Moms and dads need to learn to calm down, too!) Then you can do something fun together afterward.

After two weeks of practice, you'll be ready to use one of the slowing down methods when you're actually angry, and you'll see that it really does help you feel calmer and quieter inside.

Which method will you practice for the next two weeks?

◎ Write it here. _____

Slowing Down My Body

DAY 1	DAY 2	DAY 3	DAY 4	DAY 5	DAY 6	DAY 7
Practiced	Practiced	Practiced	Practiced	Practiced	Practiced	Practiced
☐	☐	☐	☐	☐	☐	☐

Reminder: In the second week do something active to get your heart going before you practice!

DAY 8	DAY 9	DAY 10	DAY 11	DAY 12	DAY 13	DAY 14
Practiced	Practiced	Practiced	Practiced	Practiced	Practiced	Practiced
☐	☐	☐	☐	☐	☐	☐

CHAPTER EIGHT

Anger-Dousing Method #4: Solve the Problem

When you're angry, it's as if the door that leads to the thinking part of your brain slams shut. All you can see or feel is ANGER. The part of you that knows how to be reasonable and solve problems is locked away behind that closed door. That's why the active

and slowing down methods of releasing anger are so important. They re-settle your body and re-open the door to your thinking brain, allowing you to actually deal with the problem.

Once you are thinking clearly, you'll see that when there is a problem you have two good choices. You can work it out, or you can just move on. When the door to the thinking part of your brain is fully open, you will be able to use the things you already know and the skills you're about to learn to deal with just about any problem.

Work It Out

Working a problem out means facing it head on. It means deciding to do something that will make the situation better.

In order to work the problem out, you need to be able to *assert* yourself, which means to speak up calmly and clearly. Yelling doesn't help. But talking does, especially if you use your regular voice. So the first step is to say what the problem is. That's easy. Most kids know exactly what the problem is.

So here's how that would look:

You want to stay up to watch a special show on TV, but the show is past your bedtime.

You want to ride your bike, but your friend wants to play catch.

You want to use your sister's scooter, but she won't let you.

You are working on your language arts homework, and you can't figure out what an adverb is.

The next step is to think about what you want. This is where things get a little trickier, because what you want and what is actually possible might not be the same.

That's where being flexible comes in. Being *flexible* means being able to accept something a bit different from what you originally wanted. It's a way of thinking creatively rather than staying stuck. And once you learn how to do it, you'll see that it feels good.

Here are some examples of things going wrong. In each example, what you want is different from what you can have. See if you can think of a flexible solution for each one.

You love playing football at recess, but no one remembered to bring the football.

Flexible Solution _____

_____

You are in the mood for chicken nuggets, but your family is going to a Chinese restaurant for dinner.

Flexible Solution _____

_____

You have almost beaten your video game, but your time is up and your sister is waiting for her turn.

Flexible Solution _____

_____

Now that you're thinking flexibly, go back to each of the three examples of problems and see if you can come up with two more ideas for how to solve each one. Thinking of lots of possible solutions for a problem is called *brainstorming*.

Sometimes people like the solutions you suggest, so it's easy to agree on what to do. But sometimes what you want and what the other person wants are totally different. When this happens, it's time to *compromise*.

In a compromise, everyone gets part of what they want, or something close to what they want, but not exactly what they want. Everyone gives a little and everyone gets a little to come up with a solution that has everyone feeling okay in the end. Even though you don't end up with exactly what you want, a compromise is often the best you can do. And it sure beats not solving the problem at all.

See if you can think of a compromise to solve each of these problems:

You are starving, but the rule at your house is no snacks right before meals.

Compromise _____

_____

You want to roller blade, but your friend wants to pretend you are horses.

Compromise _____

_____

You want to go outside, but your mom says it's time for homework.

Compromise _____

_____

Remember that in a compromise, no one gets exactly what they want, but everyone gets some of what they want.

When you think flexibly, brainstorm, and are willing to compromise, problems get worked out without a lot of commotion. It feels good to solve problems this way. People are happier with you, and you will feel happier, too.

Just Move On

Moving on means deciding not to keep thinking about or working on the problem, even if it hasn't really been solved. It means shrugging your shoulders and moving on to the next thing, without complaining or grumbling or holding a grudge.

For example, imagine a game of tag. You have 10 minutes of recess left, and the air is cool and it feels great to be running. You're with all of your friends, and you love playing tag, and you're It. You run like the wind, and you reach out your arm and snag someone, and now they're It, except they start arguing about whether you tagged their arm or just their sleeve, and whether it still counts. Do you really need to stop the whole game to work this out?

Probably not. It would be more fun to keep the game going, to run after someone else and tag them instead. Sometimes the best thing to do is just accept what has happened and move on.

Deciding to move on means totally letting the problem go—not exploding, not fuming in silence or holding a grudge, not brainstorming or talking it out. Moving on isn't giving up and it isn't giving in. In some situations, it's actually the smartest, most powerful thing you can do, because you're deciding not to waste your time or energy fighting against something that doesn't matter all that much.

Here are some things you can say to yourself to remind yourself that you don't have to fight every battle. See if you can think of a few more.

It feels good to learn how to shrug something off. Try it, you'll see.

It's up to you to decide when to work on solving a problem and when to just move on. In many situations, either choice is fine.

Take a look at these problems. Decide which ones you would work on by talking to the people involved and working out a solution, and which ones you would shrug off so you could move on to the next thing. Circle the words that show what you would do. Talk about your answers with the person who is reading this book with you.

**You are in line
at the water fountain,
and someone cuts
in front of you.**

Work it out   **Move on**

**Your friend promised to go
on the swings with you at recess,
but now she is playing kickball.**

Work it out   **Move on**

Your mom just got home from work, and she snaps at you for something you didn't even do.

Work it out   Move on

Your best friend told you he can't make it to your birthday party.

Work it out   Move on

You are in the middle of doing something, and your dad calls you outside to help rake.

Work it out   Move on

Your brother calls you a name just to make you mad.

Work it out   Move on

As you get better at working on problems or deciding to just move on, you'll find that you don't get angry nearly as often as you used to. Knowing that you'll be able to handle the problems that come your way makes you less likely to have those hot thoughts that used to cause so much trouble. Instead of thinking "No fair!" or "He did that on purpose!" you'll begin to think a more useful set of cool thoughts.

Take some time every day to talk to your mom or dad about a problem you handled well.

 How did you keep yourself calm?

 How did you solve the problem?

 Or did you decide to just move on?

 How did you feel afterward?

CHAPTER NINE

Recognizing Sparks

As long as you've been practicing the four anger-dousing methods, you have probably noticed that your anger doesn't flare up as quickly or get as big as it used to. It feels good, doesn't it?

That doesn't mean you never get angry, though. Everyone gets angry sometimes. One of the reasons we all get angry is that **SPARKS** continue to happen. A spark is something that sets off a reaction, like a tickle sparking the giggles or pollen sparking a sneeze. An anger spark is something that leads to hot thoughts and angry feelings.

Here are some anger sparks that other kids have listed. Put a check mark next to the ones that are sparks for you, too. Add other things that spark your anger—the feelings and situations that make you want to SCREAM.

Anger Sparks

☐ Teasing

☐ Loud chewing

☐ Losing a game

☐ Homework

☐ Feeling rushed

☐ Waking up

_____   _____

_____   _____

_____   _____

It helps to know what your own personal anger sparks are, because you might be able to keep certain ones from happening so often.

For example, if having to stop something before you're finished is a spark, try asking your parents to give you a 10-minute warning. That way you won't feel interrupted so often. Feeling interrupted might still be a spark for you, but you've done something to make it happen less frequently.

Choose one of your anger sparks, and think about whether you might be able to do something about it. Ask yourself:

◎ What is the spark?

◎ What can you do to stop this spark from happening so much?

For example:

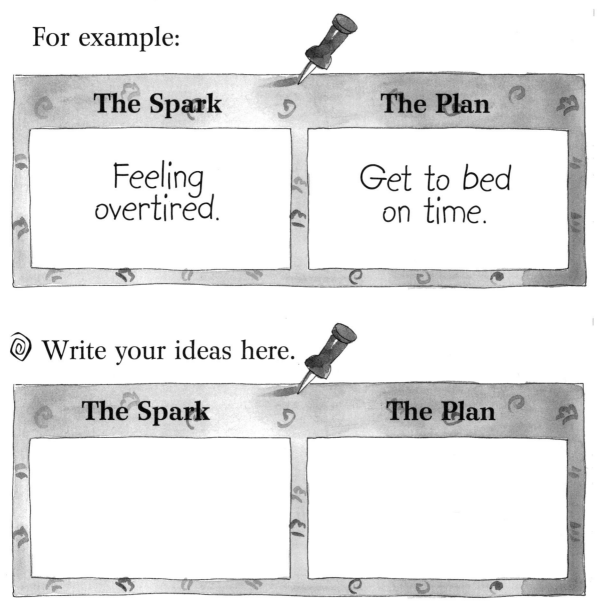

The Spark

Feeling overtired.

The Plan

Get to bed on time.

◎ Write your ideas here.

The Spark

The Plan

But some sparks can't be prevented, because they're not in your control at all, like getting teased or losing a game. For these sparks, it's a good idea to practice the cool thoughts that will help you stay calm.

For example:

The Spark	Cool Thought
When my brother calls me a baby.	He's just trying to bug me. I can still stay calm.

Choose one of the sparks that you can't stop from happening.

◎ Write it here.

The Spark	Cool Thought

When you feel angry, use one of your anger-dousing methods. Then when you're calmer, try to figure out what sparked your anger. If you notice that the same spark keeps happening over and over again, see if you can make a plan that will help you avoid that spark in the future *and* help you stay in control when it does happen.

Paybacks and Prickly Balls

You have probably noticed that some sparks just happen. Maybe you get sick on the day of your best friend's party, or maybe your theater class gets scheduled on the same day you go to your Chinese lesson. Sometimes frustrating things happen, and they aren't anyone's fault.

But some sparks are clearly someone else's fault. Your teacher assigns a ton of homework on the very same day your grandparents are coming to visit.

Or your mom doesn't get around to doing the laundry, and the shirt you want to wear is still dirty.

When someone causes a spark to happen, stop and ask yourself if they did it on purpose. Were they trying to upset you? Did your mom not do the laundry just because she didn't want you to have that shirt? Did your teacher assign homework just to get in the way of your time with your grandparents? Did they  do it just to get you mad? Lots of times, the answer to your question will be no.

When someone sets off one of your sparks, but you know they didn't do it to hurt you, you can think a cool thought, and then solve the problem or move on.

But when someone sets off one of your sparks on purpose, it's a whole different story. And that does happen sometimes. Someone does something just to be mean, to bug you, and to make you mad.

For example, you might hate being teased, and there's a kid out there—maybe your brother, maybe someone on your soccer team—who loves to tease you. Or maybe you hate it when your teacher is disappointed in you, and a kid in your class tells on you for fooling around during art.

When someone sets off one of your anger sparks, especially if it's on purpose, you might feel like getting revenge. It's tempting to think about getting back at people who hurt us. This is sometimes called a *payback*. While it might seem like paybacks even things out, they really just keep the anger going.

It's like a giant game of catch. Someone is mean to you, so you are mean back, so they are mean to you. Back and forth and back and forth you go—only the game is being played with a prickly ball. And each throw and each catch hurt!

But think about this: When someone throws a ball to you, you have a choice, right? You can catch the ball and throw it back, or you can decide not to play the game.

I'M OUT OF HERE

If you decide not to play the game, you can just let the ball drop. It's a lousy game. And you have better things to do anyway.

So instead of "catching" meanness when someone is mean to you, picture a prickly ball hurtling toward you and dropping **SPLAT!** at your feet.

There's no need to let it hit you, and there's no need to pick it up. Let the prickly ball lie there. It doesn't have to be your problem.

Think a cool thought and walk away.

Here's how this would work. Pretend you're joking around with your friends at lunch. Someone dips his finger in his pudding and puts some spots on the table. "Oooo, look," he says, "the table has chicken pox." You have some leftover ketchup on your plate, and everyone knows that chicken pox are red, so you add some red spots to make it look more real. It's not a big deal, and you were going to wipe up the mess when you were done, but another kid goes and tells on you. Now the lunch monitor is on her way over.

You remember what you've been reading in this book. So the first thing you do is think a cool thought, "I can stay calm." You realize this is a problem you need to work out, so you say you're sorry and offer to wipe down the table. After you've cleaned up, the lunch monitor makes you sit there for 5 more minutes. By the time you get outside, you've missed half of recess, but you see your friends playing wall ball and run over to join them. The kid who told on you is playing, too.

Do you slam him with the ball and pretend it was a mistake? Do you keep the ball away from him so he doesn't have any fun? Do you call him a tattletale? Do you make fun of the way he throws?

All of those are examples of paybacks, and none is the right thing to do. The best choice is to throw yourself into the game. Play it for fun. Get your heart pumping. Tell yourself that what happened in the lunchroom is over. If playing alongside that kid is too hard for now, go play kickball instead.

Deciding not to go for the payback puts you in charge in a pretty powerful way. People who think it's fun to watch you get angry, or situations that used to have you fuming, no longer have the power to upset you.

Instead, you are in the driver's seat of your own life, calmly steering away from annoyances, taking in the scenery, getting where you want to go.

Grow a Fuse

Back in the days when you used to flare up quickly, people might have said you had a "short fuse." That's another way of saying you explode quickly. It's like the dynamite you may have seen in cartoons. Sometimes there's just a tiny piece of string attached and then KABOOM! the dynamite explodes.

But sometimes cartoon dynamite has a *l-o-o-o-n-g* fuse, stretching around rocks and lakes and caves and all sorts of things. It goes on and on, and the whole length of it has to burn before anything bad happens. The main character has lots of time to do funny things, like try to outrun the explosion or set up crazy obstacles along the way.

People who have a short fuse explode quickly. But when people have a long fuse, they have time to think and breathe and decide what to do. Long fuses help people take care of their anger before it becomes too big to handle, so they can put out the fire before an explosion happens.

The methods you've learned in this book have added length to your fuse. Taking a break, thinking cool thoughts, releasing anger safely, and working out problems all stretch fuses, so explosions don't happen as quickly, or even at all.

There are other things you can do to make your fuse grow, things that are healthy and fun and can be done every day.

Getting enough exercise is a great way to lengthen your fuse. It releases stored-up tension, burning off the angry feelings that get stored in our bodies.

Playing or working hard for at least 30 minutes every day helps our bodies produce the kind of energy that makes us feel happy and strong. It can actually help us handle the problems that come our way. And besides all that, it's fun!

**Draw or write about
two exercises you can do every day.**

Eating healthy foods also stretches your fuse. Just like the right fuel in a car makes the engine run smoothly, good food helps your body run smoothly. And when you're running at your best, you're in better shape to handle obstacles in the road.

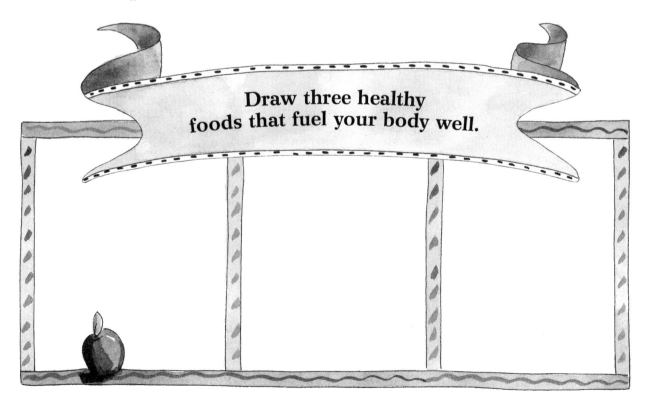

**Draw three healthy
foods that fuel your body well.**

Getting enough sleep is a fuse-builder, too. When you're well rested, it's easier to stay calm and handle disappointments. Kids need between 9 and 11 hours of sleep every night.

◎Mark the time you go to sleep on school days...

...and the time you wake up.

◎How many hours of sleep are you getting?

◎If you aren't getting enough, talk to your parents about a plan to help you get the sleep your body needs.

Having free time and doing fun things keep fuses long, too, because being relaxed and enjoying life help you handle bumps in the road—the frustrating, disappointing, unfair things that happen to all of us.

Draw something you do for fun.

CHAPTER TWELVE

You Can Do It!

You are becoming an expert in managing your anger. And if you've been practicing everything you've learned, you are spending lots of time in the driver's seat of your own life.

You are able to stay on course even when things aren't going your way. You know how to steer around problems or work them out. And you stay in control of yourself, even when the going is tough.

Congratulations.

You might be interested to know that the anger-dousing methods you've learned aren't just for kids. They are the same methods that are used by the adults you admire, the ones who are calm and funny and nice, who don't explode when something goes wrong.

You can use these methods for the rest of your life. You can grow up to be an adult that kids admire, an adult who is calm and funny and nice.

All you need to do is remember to use your anger-dousing methods:

Anger-Dousing Methods

◎ **Take a break.**

◎ **Think cool thoughts.**

◎ **Release anger safely.**

◎ **Work it out or just move on.**

It feels good to be in control of yourself. Being in control makes it easier to get where you want to go, and to enjoy the scenery along the way.